The Power of Time Management and Goal Setting for Academic Success

IT CERTS TRAINING

By Robert Cabeca

Founder,

IT Certs Training, LLC

www.itcertstraining.com

Special Offer: Act Now!

Thank you for taking the time to get and read this powerful book on goal setting and time management!

This book will guide you to reaching your academic achievement!

To support you in this, if you have not yet already become a member of IT Certs Training, please **use this code** right now to get **15% off** your new course bundle now!

https://ITCERTSTRAINING.COM

15OFFBOOKOFFER

(Copy and paste the above code into your shopping cart)

- Blast past fear and resistance
- Embrace your academic and career goals
- Harness your inner energy to rocket you to your dreams
- Achieve your desired goals effortlessly and expeditiously!

Copyright

Preface

Why be concerned with time management when studying to achieve an academic goal?

You won't necessarily fail if you don't.

But, your life and sanity, will be so much happier!

You will have more time to spend doing other things you love!

You will succeed faster and more resoundingly!

History Lesson: I had just started my first business at 18. And I just moved to Washington, DC. I had just enrolled in an engineering degree at University of D.C. I just moved into my own apartment. And I was working a full-time job as a server. And I had just got into a wonderful relationship.

Life was wonderful! And then it all got out of control. Sadly, I had to drop out of school. Lost my boyfriend and was about to lose my fabulous apartment on Capital Hill. Which I did.

What the heck happened??? And how did it all happen so fast and seemingly without my knowing?

I thought I could manage everything that was going on, on my own. Without help. Without feedback. Without guidance.

Anyone who tried to help got shunned.

Not a great story so far, is it?

I had goals, but they were lofty and existed only in my mind. I did not attempt to develop a study schedule, or a set work schedule. I wanted to spend all my free time with my boyfriend, who was enrolled in George Washington University. And I needed money to pay bills, have fun and live. Makes sense, right?

Well, my boyfriend was doing something I was not: Mark was keeping track of his schedule, his assignment due dates, his upcoming exams and managed his time to the point where he was able to tell me what times and days during the coming week he could get together with me and go out.

How rude of him I thought!

Mark graduated with a 4.0 from GWU.

I dropped out because I was not willing to set goals, track my goal progress, turn in my assignments on time, etc, etc, etc.

Mark dropped me because I kept wanting him to spend time with me when his schedule was set to study and do assignments. In my mind, his school was more important than me!

Seriously?

What could possibly be more important than me? Right?

I disrespected his commitment to his education, his goals and his life. Though he truly loved me and wanted me as a part of his life, he saw that not only did I disrespect him, but I was also disrespecting myself and my life by not following my own commitments to my own goals.

Lesson learned. Painfully.

Rinse, but do not repeat!

Since that time, I have learned life changing transformational time management and goal setting strategies that rapidly materialize the dreams and goals of someone's life!

I am here to teach them to you, **now**.

How can I vouch that these strategies work?

I know they work because I own 11 (eleven) business right now. One of those is as an executive business and life coach, which means I meet with clients almost every day of the week. I am also a professional artist and musician and writer. I also produce TV shows. I avidly exercise. I love to cook and eat great food every day. I have time to meditate and write and enjoy my life, every day. And, I have no employees to do the grunt work for me.

My goals are clear and defined. My time is managed so I can be both successful and life a full and enjoyable life.

Table of Contents

Chapter 1: Introduction

The Importance of Time Management and Goal Setting

Time management and goal setting are essential skills for anyone wanting to excel at achieving their academic aspirations. With the ever-increasing demands of daily life, it's crucial to effectively manage your time and set clear, achievable goals to make the most of a successful learning journey!

In today's fast-paced world, everyone faces a myriad of distractions, commitments, and responsibilities that can easily derail your academic progress. Time management serves as a guiding compass, enabling you to navigate through the complexities of your academic life while maintaining a healthy balance between studying and other activities.

By mastering time management, you can optimize your study sessions, allocate sufficient time for leisure, and fulfill social obligations without compromising your academic performance. Effective time management empowers you to prioritize tasks, focus on what truly matters, and avoid the trap of procrastination, ensuring that you consistently make progress towards your goals.

Furthermore, goal setting provides a clear roadmap for your academic journey. When you have well-defined and measurable objectives, you create a sense of purpose that fuels your motivation and determination. As you achieve these milestones, you build confidence in your abilities and develop a positive mindset that propels you towards even greater accomplishments.

Here are some key benefits of time management and goal setting for students:

1. Enhanced Productivity: By organizing your study schedule and breaking tasks into manageable chunks, you can complete more work in less time, leaving you with additional opportunities to explore other interests and activities.

2. Reduced Stress: Proper time management allows you to stay on top of your academic responsibilities, minimizing the last-minute rush and avoiding the anxiety associated with missed deadlines.

3. Improved Academic Performance: Setting clear goals helps you focus on your studies and identify areas that require attention. This, in turn, fosters better learning outcomes and academic results.

4. Increased Focus and Concentration: Time management techniques, such as the Pomodoro Technique, enable you to maintain high levels of focus during study sessions, enhancing your understanding and retention of the material.

5. Better Work-Life Balance: Effective time management ensures that you allocate time for both academic pursuits and personal interests, allowing you to lead a more balanced and fulfilling life.

6. Greater Sense of Accomplishment: As you achieve your goals and make progress towards larger aspirations, you experience a sense of accomplishment that boosts your confidence and motivation.

7. Long-Term Vision: Goal setting encourages you to envision your future and identify the steps needed to reach your desired academic and career objectives.

8. Adaptability and Resilience: Time management and goal setting teach you to be adaptable and make necessary adjustments in your approach to achieve success in the face of changing circumstances or challenges.

It's important to note that time management and goal setting are not one-size-fits-all approaches. Each student has their unique learning style, personal preferences, and strengths. Therefore, it's essential to experiment with the different strategies I this book and tailor them to suit your individual needs.

In the following chapters, we will delve deeper into the principles of time management and goal setting, providing you with practical techniques and tools to not only enhance your studying and learning experience, but to also help ensure your academic success. By the end of this eBook, you will have a comprehensive toolkit to optimize your time, set meaningful goals, overcome obstacles, pass exams, and embark on a successful academic journey filled with achievements and personal growth.

Let's begin this transformative process together!

Benefits of Effective Time Management

Discover the numerous benefits of effective time management, including reduced stress, improved productivity, better work-life balance, and the ability to stay focused on your academic objectives.

Effective time management not only allows you to accomplish your immediate tasks and goals efficiently but also opens up doors for personal growth and development.

When you manage your time effectively, you create a supportive environment that encourages continuous learning and self-improvement through focus and concentration. Here are some ways in which time management can contribute to your personal development:

1. **Time for Learning:** With a well-organized schedule, you can allocate dedicated time for learning new skills, acquiring knowledge, or pursuing educational courses. Whether it's taking an online class, attending workshops, or reading educational books, effective time management ensures that you make learning a priority amidst your other responsibilities.

2. **Goal Setting and Achievement:** Time management helps you set realistic and achievable goals, breaking them down into smaller tasks with specific deadlines. As you accomplish these milestones, you experience a sense of accomplishment and motivation, propelling you forward towards more significant achievements in both your academic and personal life.

3. **Focus and Concentration:** Being able to set time based goals heightens your ability to focus clearly and accurately. When you focus your attention you are able to concentrate your thoughts on specific learning topics which allows your brain to do what it does best: create neural pathways between ideas that create memory retention and recollection.

4. **Self-Reflection and Improvement:** Allocating time for self-reflection becomes possible when you manage your time effectively. Regularly evaluating your progress, strengths, and weaknesses helps you identify areas that need improvement, allowing you to work on personal development with intention.

5. **Health and Well-being:** Effective time management not only reduces stress but also allows you to prioritize self-care. You can make time for regular exercise, meditation, or engaging in hobbies you enjoy. A healthy work-life balance contributes to your overall well-being, ensuring you stay physically and mentally fit to tackle challenges effectively.

6. **Expanding Your Network:** Time management enables you to allocate time for professional networking and building meaningful relationships. Meeting new people, attending conferences, or participating in community events can expose you to diverse perspectives and open doors to new opportunities. Additionally, many students thrive with accountability partners, which can usually be found through these great relationships.

7. **Exploring New Interests:** When you manage your time efficiently, you create room to explore new interests and passions outside your academic pursuits. Trying out new activities or hobbies can spark creativity, reduce monotony, and add more depth to your personal experiences in addition to enhancing your learning abilities.

8. **Enhanced Adaptability:** As you learn to manage your time effectively, you become more adaptable and resilient. When unexpected challenges arise, you are better equipped to adjust your schedule, prioritize tasks, and navigate through uncertain situations. You can easily say "yes" or "no" to things without regret because you are now basing your decisions on clear goals.

9. **Time for Reflection and Relaxation:** Effective time management allows you to build time into your day for natural relaxation and mental rejuvenation. Your brain requires downtime in order to keep up with your learning pace. Moments of quiet contemplation, meditation or mindfulness, help you gain clarity about your long-term goals, values, and aspirations. This fosters personal growth and a stronger sense of purpose and direction in your life. Overstimulation, or forced artificial downtime (through alcohol or drugs), quickly depletes your brain's ability to retain and recall newly learned information.

10. **Increased Productivity:** By managing your time wisely, you can accomplish your studying tasks more efficiently and quickly, leaving more room for personal development initiatives. Increased productivity gives you the freedom to invest time in activities that align with your passions and goals. When you feel you have this freedom, the stress of studying and passing exams falls away, making it significantly easier for you to study and pass exams!

11. **Cultivating Discipline and Focus:** The word "Discipline" has a bad rap usually. It simply means to be a committed student to learning a new skill or enhancing knowledge. Developing effective time management habits requires commitment. As you practice these new skills, they flow into other aspects of your life, such as maintaining focus during study sessions and passing exams.

In conclusion, effective time management lays the foundation of your successful academic journey. You will be completing tasks and meeting deadlines quickly and efficiently. As a valuable tool that can unlock numerous benefits for personal growth and development, you can harness the power of time management, create a fulfilling and well-rounded life, embrace opportunities to learn, explore, and evolve as an individual. Remember, time is a finite resource, and managing it effectively is key to making the most of every moment in your academic journey and beyond.

The Power of Goal Setting in Academic Success

Understand the connection between goal setting and learning. Learning how setting well-defined goals can provide direction, motivation, and a sense of accomplishment in your academic pursuits. Especially passing exams.

In the previous section, we explored the fundamental relationship between Time Management and learning. We discovered how well-defined goals can serve as guiding beacons, igniting motivation, and fostering a sense of accomplishment in your academic journey.

Now, let's delve deeper into the remarkable power of goal setting and how it directly influences academic success. By understanding and harnessing this power, you can pave the way for rapid transformative learning experiences and propel yourself towards excellence.

Direction and Clarity

Imagine embarking on a journey without a map or a destination in mind. It would be a daunting and confusing task, as you wouldn't know where to begin or which path to take. Similarly, when you approach your studies without clear goals, you risk wandering aimlessly, unsure of what you want to achieve... or the steps to get there.

Setting well-defined goals provides much-needed direction and clarity to your academic pursuits. Goals act as a compass, pointing you towards the desired destination, and outlining the most efficient route to reach it. Well-defined help you prioritize tasks, allocate time wisely, and stay focused on what truly matters.

Incorporating consistent goal setting into your regular learning routine enables you to break down larger objectives into smaller, manageable and achievable tasks. By doing so, you avoid feeling overwhelmed and increase your chances of success. Whether it's mastering a complex subject, acing an exam, or completing a research project, having clearly defined goals ensures you always have a clear vision of where you're headed and how you will get there, on time.

Motivation and Perseverance

At times, maintaining motivation in the face of challenges can be an uphill battle. The path of learning is often sprinkled with obstacles, such as difficult concepts, time constraints, and occasional setbacks. It's during these moments that the power of goal setting truly shines.

When you set specific, achievable goals, you create a *psychological framework* that fuels your motivation. By envisioning the rewards and benefits of achieving your objectives, you ignite an *intrinsic drive* to persist in your efforts. This unwavering determination becomes the engine that propels you forward, even when the going gets tough or seems impossible. You will find the way to keep moving forward.

Moreover, the act of setting goals itself can serve as a catalyst for motivation. The process of planning and visualizing your future accomplishments triggers a surge of enthusiasm and excitement. It's like laying the foundation for a building; once the blueprint is in place, you become eager to see the structure take shape. But you cannot create what you cannot see, and clear well-defined goals is the vision you build from.

A Sense of Accomplishment

One of the most satisfying feelings in life is experiencing a sense of accomplishment.

It's that moment, when you look back at your actions, and realize how far you've really come. Goal setting amplifies this feeling by providing a roadmap to track your progress and celebrate your achievements along the way.

As you reach and surpass milestones in your academic journey, you gain confidence and a sense of self-efficacy: more assurance in your abilities and belief in your capacity to tackle even more significant challenges. This new-found confidence becomes a powerful beneficial cycle, driving you to set even more ambitious goals and surpass your previous accomplishments.

Embrace SMART Goals

(More specific details about SMART Goals is defined later in the book)

To maximize the benefits of goal setting, it's essential to embrace a framework that enhances their effectiveness. One such framework is SMART goals:

1. Specific: Clearly define what you want to achieve. Avoid vague aspirations and focus on precise outcomes.

2. Measurable: Set criteria to measure your progress and determine when the goal has been accomplished.

3. Achievable: Ensure that your goals are realistic and attainable with the resources and time available.

4. Relevant: Align your goals with your broader academic aspirations and ensure they contribute meaningfully to your growth.

5. Time-bound: Set deadlines for your goals to create a sense of urgency and prevent procrastination.

Goal setting is a potent tool that enhances learning and studying in numerous ways. By providing direction, motivation, and a sense of accomplishment, well-defined goals elevate your academic experience to new heights. Embrace the power of goal setting in your educational journey, and you will discover the transformative impact it can have on your path to academic success.

Chapter 2: Understanding Time Management

Assessing Your Time Management Skills

Take a self-assessment to identify your current time management strengths and weaknesses. By understanding where you stand, you can tailor your approach to suit your needs.

Identifying Your Time Management Style with a Habit Finder Assessment

Previously we discussed the importance of assessing your time management skills to gain insights into your strengths and weaknesses. Now, we will delve deeper into the process of identifying your resourceful and unresourceful habits using a powerful tool known as the Habit Finder Assessment. https://habitfindercoach.com/deep

What is a Habit Finder Assessment?

The Habit Finder Assessment is a specialized tool designed to help individuals gain a better understanding of their unique habits and tendencies. It assesses various aspects of your thought patterns to provide you with personalized insights. By identifying your dominant thought habits, you can leverage them to optimize your time management and productivity and sense of joy and fulfillment in your life.

How to Take the Habit Finder Assessment

1. Visit https://habitfindercoach.com/deep: Start by taking the Habit Finder Assessment online.

2. Answer Thoughtful Questions: Set aside about 15 minutes to take the assessment. Ideally, take the assessment first thing in the morning before you get your day started. You will be presented with a series of thought-provoking statements about your preferences. Take your time to answer these questions honestly and introspectively.

3. Avoid Overthinking: It's essential to respond instinctively rather than overthinking your answers. The assessment aims to capture your natural inclinations, so trust your gut feelings when responding.

4. Review Your Results: After completing the assessment, you will receive a detailed report outlining your thought habits. This report will shed light on your strengths and weaknesses related to joy, relationships, time management, goal-setting, decision-making, and more.

Interpreting the Habit Finder Results for Time Management Improvement

Once you have your Habit Finder Assessment results in hand, it's time to interpret them and apply the insights to your life. You will receive a link to schedule a debrief session to better understand your results. Here are some key areas to focus on:

1. Time Management Preferences: The assessment may reveal whether you are more inclined towards structure and routine or prefer a flexible and spontaneous approach. This knowledge can guide you in setting up a time management system that aligns with your preferences.

2. Procrastination Triggers: Understanding the factors that contribute to procrastination is vital for overcoming this common productivity roadblock. The assessment might identify your specific triggers, allowing you to develop strategies to combat procrastination effectively.

3. Goal-Setting Strategies: Time management and goal-setting go hand in hand. Your Habit Finder results can help you identify the most effective strategies for setting and pursuing your goals. Whether you thrive with short-term objectives or prefer long-term planning, this knowledge will refine your goal-setting process.

4. Task Prioritization: Prioritizing tasks is a critical skill for effective time management. The assessment can highlight whether you tend to prioritize based on urgency, importance, or other factors. This insight will enable you to allocate your time and energy more efficiently.

5. Time Perception: Your perception of time passing can significantly impact your time management. If you have a tendency to underestimate or overestimate time, the assessment results can help you adjust your time allocation for tasks accordingly.

6. Time Wasting Patterns: Identifying your time-wasting patterns is essential for improving productivity. The Habit Finder Assessment may pinpoint areas where you tend to lose focus or engage in non-productive activities, allowing you to address these behaviors.

7. Stress and Time Management: Stress can affect how you manage your time. The assessment results may indicate if you are more prone to stress-related time management challenges, such as time pressure or difficulty managing multiple tasks simultaneously.

Remember that the Habit Finder Assessment is a tool for self-awareness and improvement. Embrace the results with an open mind.

Don't forget to schedule your *free* strategy and debriefing session after you get your results!

Identifying Time Wasters and Time Management Strategies

Uncover common time-wasting habits and distractions that hinder your studying efforts. Learn how to overcome these challenges and create a more productive study environment.

Now that you have completed the self-assessment and gained valuable insights from the Habit Finder Assessment, it's time to tailor your time management strategies. In this chapter, we will explore effective time management techniques based on various habit tendencies.

1. Structured Scheduling:

To optimize your time management, consider the following strategies:

a. Establish Clear Routines: Embrace your inclination for structure by creating daily, weekly, and monthly routines. Having a consistent schedule helps you allocate time effectively and ensures that essential tasks receive the attention they deserve.

b. Prioritize with Purpose: Make a to-do list at the end of the day or at the beginning of each day, prioritizing tasks based on importance and deadlines. Stick to your schedule as much as possible, but allow for flexibility when unexpected tasks arise.

c. Time Blocking: (described further in this book) Implement time blocking techniques to dedicate specific time slots for focused work on individual tasks. By assigning blocks of time for different activities, you can maintain your productivity and prevent distractions.

d. Set Realistic Goals: While your disciplined nature may encourage setting ambitious goals, ensure they are achievable within a given timeframe. Break larger tasks into smaller, manageable milestones to track your progress effectively.

2. Adaptable Improvisation:

Flexibility and spontaneity are strong resources. To harness your time management potential, consider these strategies:

a. Embrace Flexibility: Allow room for improvisation in your schedule. While having a loose structure is fine, make sure you allocate enough time for essential tasks and responsibilities.

b. Agile Task Management: Embrace agile task management techniques, such as Kanban boards or electronic task management tools. These methods allow you to adjust priorities and tackle tasks as they come, making the most of your adaptive nature.

c. Take Breaks Strategically: At times it might be easy to get engrossed in tasks for extended periods. Breaks are essential for recharging and maintaining focus. Schedule short breaks to relax and rejuvenate during intense work sessions. (see the Pomodoro technique later in the book)

d. Leverage Spontaneous Creativity: Your ability to think on your feet can lead to innovative solutions. Channel your spontaneous creativity when problem-solving or brainstorming new ideas.

3. Specialized Focus:

Learn to utilize deep concentration and attention to detail to excel in your activites. To optimize your time management, consider the following strategies:

a. Utilize the Pomodoro Technique: The Pomodoro Technique involves working in focused intervals (typically 25 minutes) followed by short breaks. Use this method to maintain your concentration and prevent burnout.

b. Minimize Distractions: Create a distraction-free environment to make the most of your focused work style. Turn off unnecessary notifications and consider using website blockers during intense work sessions.

c. Set Specific Goals: As a focused specialist, you may find satisfaction in diving deep into a single task. Define clear and specific goals for each task to maintain your sense of accomplishment.

d. Avoid Overcommitment: Be mindful of your tendency to get absorbed in tasks. Avoid taking on too many responsibilities simultaneously to prevent feeling overwhelmed.

4. Visions and Creating Dreams:

Creativity and big-picture thinking are real strengths. To enhance your time management, consider these strategies:

a. Goal Visualization: Use your imaginative (not fantastical) abilities to visualize your long-term goals vividly. Keep a vision board or a digital visual representation to remind yourself of your aspirations.

b. Break Down Goals: While you might be excellent at envisioning grand plans, breaking them down into actionable steps is crucial. Divide larger projects into smaller tasks and set realistic deadlines for each.

c. Delegate and Collaborate: As a visionary, you may have many ideas, but executing them all alone can be overwhelming. Learn to delegate tasks or collaborate with others who can help bring your ideas to life.

d. Time for Creative Exploration: Schedule designated time for creative exploration and brainstorming sessions. Give your visionary mind space to wander and generate new ideas.

5. Analytical Strategies:

Data-driven decision-making and critical thinking are real assets. To optimize your time management, consider these strategies:

a. Analyze Time Usage: Use your analytical skills to assess how you spend your time each day. Identify areas where you can make improvements and streamline your routines.

b. Use Productivity Tools: Leverage time-tracking apps or productivity software to monitor your progress on tasks and projects. Analyzing the data can help you optimize your time allocation.

c. Evaluate Task Importance: Prioritize tasks based on their impact and align them with your long-term goals. Avoid getting bogged down by trivial matters that don't contribute significantly to your objectives.

d. Continuous Improvement: You may find joy in constantly refining your processes. Embrace a mindset of continuous improvement, always seeking ways to enhance your time management techniques.

By recognizing and adapting your habit tendencies, you can supercharge your time management skills. Remember that these habits are not rigid categories, and you may possess characteristics from more than one type. Embrace your uniqueness, experiment with various strategies, and find what works best for you.

Techniques for Effective Time Management

Explore various time management techniques, such as the 80/20 rule, time blocking, and task prioritization, to optimize your schedule and enhance your learning experience.

Mastering Time Management for Enhanced Productivity

Mastering time management is crucial for both personal and professional success. In this chapter, we will delve deeper into some effective time management techniques that will not only optimize your schedule but also significantly enhance your learning experience. By implementing these strategies, you can achieve more in less time and create a harmonious balance between your educational pursuits and other commitments.

1. The 80/20 Rule (Pareto Principle):

The 80/20 rule, also known as the Pareto Principle, states that 80% of your results come from 20% of your efforts. In the context of time management and learning, this means that a significant portion of your academic achievements can be attributed to a few key activities or subjects. To apply the 80/20 rule to your studies, follow these steps:

a. Identify the critical 20%: Analyze your academic journey and determine the subjects or tasks that have the most significant impact on your grades and overall knowledge.

b. Focus on high-priority activities: Once you identify the vital subjects, allocate more time and energy to study and master them. This will enable you to make significant strides in your learning journey.

c. Reduce non-essential tasks: Recognize the activities that are not contributing much to your academic progress and find ways to delegate or reduce them. This way, you free up time for more valuable pursuits.

2. Time Blocking:

Time blocking is an effective technique that involves dividing your day into specific blocks of time dedicated to particular tasks. By assigning fixed time slots for studying, leisure, and other responsibilities, you create a structured routine that minimizes distractions and enhances productivity. Here's how you can implement time blocking for your studies:

a. Plan your day ahead: Each evening or early morning, plan your schedule for the day, allotting specific time blocks for studying various subjects, attending lectures, and engaging in extracurricular activities.

b. Stick to the schedule: Once you've created a time block, commit to following it diligently. Avoid distractions during these blocks and focus solely on the task at hand.

c. Be flexible but disciplined: While it's essential to be adaptable to unforeseen circumstances, maintain discipline in adhering to the time blocks you've set. This will help you make steady progress in your studies.

3. Task Prioritization:

Effective task prioritization is vital for managing your time efficiently. When you have multiple assignments, projects, and activities to tackle, it's essential to prioritize them based on their importance and deadlines. Follow these steps to prioritize tasks effectively:

a. Create an action list: Start each day by listing all the tasks you need to accomplish. This will help you have a clear overview of your responsibilities.

b. Identify urgent and important tasks: Categorize your tasks based on their urgency and significance. Focus on the ones that have imminent deadlines or carry more weight in your academic performance.

c. Use tools and techniques: Various tools, such as the Eisenhower Matrix (dividing tasks into four quadrants based on urgency and importance), can aid you in effectively prioritizing your tasks.

d. Celebrate accomplishments: As you complete tasks, take a moment to acknowledge your progress. Celebrating small achievements will boost your motivation to tackle the next task.

4. The Pomodoro Technique:

The Pomodoro Technique is a time management method developed by Francesco Cirillo. It involves breaking your work or study time into intervals, typically 25 minutes long, separated by short breaks. This technique can be highly effective for maintaining focus and avoiding burnout during intense study sessions.

a. Set a timer for 25 minutes: Choose a task or subject to study and set a timer for 25 minutes. This time period is called a "Pomodoro."

b. Work with complete focus: During the 25 minutes, concentrate solely on the task at hand, avoiding distractions and interruptions.

c. Take a short break: Once the Pomodoro is complete, take a 5-minute break to recharge and relax your mind.

d. Repeat and take longer breaks: After completing four Pomodoros, take a more extended break of about 15-30 minutes to rejuvenate before resuming your study sessions.

Conclusion:

Effective time management is an invaluable skill that will not only optimize your schedule but also enrich your learning experience. By incorporating techniques like the 80/20 rule, time blocking, task prioritization, and the Pomodoro Technique into your daily routine, you can achieve more with less effort. Remember, consistency and discipline are key to mastering these time management techniques and unlocking your full academic potential. Embrace these strategies, and you'll find yourself excelling in your studies while still having time for other pursuits that bring you joy and fulfillment.

Chapter 3: Setting SMART Goals for Studying and Learning

What Are SMART Goals?

Learn about the SMART goal-setting framework (Specific, Measurable, Attainable, Relevant, Time-Bound) and how it can help you set clear and achievable objectives for your studies.

Attaining a Certification using SMART Goals

In the constantly evolving field of cybersecurity, certifications play a vital role in validating the skills and knowledge of professionals. A SMART approach to setting goals can significantly enhance your chances of obtaining a cybersecurity certification successfully. In this chapter, we will dive deep into each component of SMART—Specific, Measurable, Achievable, Relevant, and Time-bound—to help you create and implement effective goals for attaining a cybersecurity certification.

Defining Specific Goals

When setting specific goals for a cybersecurity certification, it's essential to be precise about what you want to achieve. General aspirations like "obtaining a cybersecurity certification" won't cut it. Instead, identify a specific certification that aligns with your career objectives, such as the Certified Information Systems Security Professional (CISSP) or Certified Ethical Hacker (CEH) certification.

Identify the Target Certification:

Research different certifications and select the one that best suits your interests, experience, and career path. Each certification focuses on distinct areas of cybersecurity, so pick the one that aligns with your expertise and future goals.

Set Clear Objectives:

Break down the certification process into smaller, achievable objectives. For instance, if the certification requires passing an exam, set a goal for the number of hours you'll study each day or week.

Measuring Success with Measurable Goals

Measuring progress is crucial for staying on track and motivated. Measurable goals provide tangible evidence of your achievements and help you identify areas that require more effort.

Track Study Hours:

Allocate a specific number of hours each week for studying and preparing for the certification exam. Keep a detailed record of the time you spend on various topics to ensure you stay consistent.

Take Practice Exams:

Regularly take practice exams to gauge your knowledge and identify weak points. Set a target score for each practice test, and work diligently to improve your performance over time.

Making Goals Achievable

While ambitious goals are essential for growth, they must also be realistic and attainable. Failing to achieve unrealistic objectives can lead to frustration and demotivation.

Assess Your Current Knowledge:

Evaluate your existing cybersecurity skills and knowledge to determine the level of preparation needed for the certification. Be honest about your strengths and weaknesses and focus on enhancing areas where you lack proficiency.

Consider Professional Training:

If you feel that self-study might not be sufficient, explore **reputable training programs** or courses that align with the certification requirements. Investing in quality training can provide valuable insights and boost your chances of success.

Ensuring Relevance in Goal Setting

Ensure that the certification you pursue is relevant to your career aspirations and industry demand. A certification that aligns with your professional goals will not only enhance your resume but also improve your expertise in the areas that interest you the most.

Industry Trends:

Research the current and future trends in cybersecurity to understand which certifications are most relevant and sought after by employers. Stay up-to-date with the latest threats, technologies, and best practices.

Career Advancement:

Consider how the certification fits into your long-term career plans. Will it open new opportunities, lead to promotions, or enhance your earning potential?

Setting Time-Bound Goals

Setting a deadline for achieving your cybersecurity certification is essential for maintaining focus and discipline. A time-bound goal creates a sense of urgency and prevents procrastination.

Exam Registration Deadline:

Check the certification exam schedule and set a target date for registration. This will give you a clear timeframe for exam preparation.

Study Schedule:

Develop a study plan with specific milestones and deadlines leading up to the exam date. Break down the material into manageable chunks and allocate ample time for review.

Incorporating SMART goal-setting principles into your cybersecurity certification journey will significantly improve your chances of success. Remember to be specific about your objectives, track your progress, set realistic targets, choose relevant certifications, and establish a clear timeline for achieving your goals. By following this framework, you'll be better equipped to overcome challenges and advance your career in the dynamic and rewarding field of cybersecurity. Good luck on your certification journey!

Chapter 4: Creating a Productive Study Environment

The Power of a Well-Optimized Study Environment

Discover how your study environment can impact your focus, productivity, and overall learning experience.

Creating an ideal study environment is more than just finding a quiet corner or a comfortable chair. It involves carefully curating the space to optimize your focus, productivity, and overall learning experience. In this chapter, we will delve deeper into the key factors that contribute to a well-optimized study environment and how it can positively influence your learning journey.

1. Declutter for Clarity

A cluttered study environment can be overwhelming and distracting. When your study space is cluttered with unnecessary items, your brain may struggle to filter out distractions, making it harder to concentrate. To combat this, take some time to declutter your study area regularly. Keep only the essentials within reach and remove any items that are unrelated to your study tasks.

2. Light Up Your Mind

Proper lighting is essential for maintaining focus and preventing eye strain. Natural light is ideal whenever possible, as it positively impacts mood and helps regulate your internal body clock. Position your study desk near a window to allow in natural light during the day. In the evenings or in spaces with limited natural light, opt for adjustable artificial lighting that is neither too dim nor too bright.

3. The Right Ergonomics

Your physical comfort plays a significant role in your ability to concentrate and learn effectively. Poor ergonomics can lead to discomfort, back pain, and reduced productivity. Invest in an ergonomic chair that supports good posture and a desk that allows your arms to rest comfortably while typing or writing. Position your computer screen at eye level to reduce strain on your neck and eyes.

4. Choose the Right Colors

Believe it or not, the colors in your study environment can influence your mood and cognitive performance. Different colors evoke various emotions, so it's essential to choose wisely. For example, blue and green are often associated with calmness and focus, while red can stimulate alertness and attention to detail. Incorporate colors that complement your study goals and personal preferences.

5. Silence or Ambient Sounds?

The impact of sound on learning varies from person to person. Some individuals work best in complete silence, while others prefer soft background music or ambient sounds. Experiment with different auditory settings to find what works best for you. If you choose to listen to music, opt for instrumental or lyric-free tracks to minimize distractions.

6. Embrace Nature

Bringing elements of nature into your study environment can have a positive impact on your cognitive function. Adding some potted plants or a small indoor garden not only enhances the aesthetics of your space but also improves air quality and reduces stress levels. Nature-inspired decor can create a calming atmosphere that supports your learning process.

7. Keep It Organized

Organization is the key to efficiency. Keep your study materials, books, and notes well-organized and easily accessible. Consider using shelves, drawers, or storage containers to maintain order in your study area. An organized environment reduces the time wasted searching for materials and fosters a clear and structured mindset.

8. Limit Digital Distractions

While technology can be a valuable learning tool, it can also be a source of distraction. Avoid the temptation of constantly checking social media, email, or other unrelated websites during study sessions. Use website blockers or apps that limit your access to distracting websites during dedicated study hours.

9. Personalize Your Space

Make your study environment your own by personalizing it with items that motivate and inspire you. Displaying motivational quotes, pictures of loved ones, or achievements can remind you of your goals and keep you focused on your studies.

10. Flexibility and Adaptability

Lastly, remember that the study environment is not a one-size-fits-all concept. Your needs and preferences may change over time, so be open to adaptability. If you find that your current study environment is not as effective as it used to be, don't hesitate to make adjustments and improvements.

Conclusion

Your study environment plays a crucial role in shaping your learning experience. By optimizing your study space to reduce distractions, improve comfort, and enhance your overall well-being, you can significantly boost your focus, productivity, and knowledge retention. Remember, creating an ideal study environment is a personal journey, so take the time to experiment and find what works best for you. With a well-optimized study environment, you'll be well-equipped to conquer your educational pursuits and achieve your learning goals.

Chapter 5: Developing Effective Study Habits

Understanding Your Learning Style

Identify your preferred learning style and adapt your study techniques to suit your unique way of absorbing information.

In the previous chapter, we discussed the importance of understanding your learning style to maximize your study efforts. Now, it's time to delve deeper into the various learning styles and identify which one resonates with you the most. Remember, everyone has a unique way of absorbing information, and recognizing your learning style will help you tailor your study techniques for optimal results.

1. Visual Learners:

If you are a visual learner, you process information best through images, diagrams, and visual aids. You have a keen eye for details, and your memory is often triggered by colors, shapes, and patterns. Here are some study techniques that align with your learning style:

a. Mind Maps: Create colorful and visually appealing mind maps to organize complex concepts. Use different colors, arrows, and icons to connect related ideas and make your study material more engaging.

b. Flashcards: Design flashcards with pictures and graphics to associate information with visual cues. This method helps reinforce your memory and facilitates easy recall during exams.

c. Infographics: Seek out educational infographics related to your subject matter. They present information in a visually appealing manner, making it easier for you to comprehend and retain information.

2. Auditory Learners:

As an auditory learner, you learn best through sound and verbal communication. You have a strong ability to remember information presented in the form of lectures, discussions, or audio recordings. Here are some study techniques that suit your learning style:

a. Record Lectures: If possible, record lectures or study group discussions to listen to them later. Replaying the audio will reinforce your understanding of the material and help you remember key points.

b. Explaining Out Loud: Engage in conversations about the subject matter with peers or even yourself. Verbalizing information will reinforce your understanding and enhance your memory retention.

c. Rhymes and Mnemonics: Create rhymes, songs, or mnemonic devices to remember important facts, dates, or formulas. The rhythmic patterns will make the information more memorable for you.

3. Kinesthetic Learners:

Kinesthetic learners, also known as tactile learners, thrive through hands-on experiences and physical activities. You prefer learning by doing and may find it challenging to sit still during long study sessions. Here are some study techniques tailored to your learning style:

a. Hands-On Activities: Engage in experiments, simulations, or practical exercises related to your subject. This will help you grasp complex concepts through direct experience.

b. Role-Playing: If applicable to your study material, try role-playing scenarios to understand real-life applications and implications. This method enables you to connect theoretical knowledge with practical situations.

c. Study Breaks: Take regular study breaks to incorporate physical activities like stretching, walking, or even doodling. These breaks will help keep you energized and maintain focus during your study sessions.

4. Reading/Writing Learners:

Reading/Writing learners excel in absorbing information through the written word. You enjoy reading books, taking notes, and expressing your thoughts through writing. Here are some study techniques tailored to your learning style:

a. Note-Taking: Create detailed and organized notes during lectures or while reading textbooks. Summarize key points, highlight essential information, and make use of bullet points for clarity.

b. Rewriting Information: Transcribe or rewrite complex concepts in your own words. This process helps reinforce your understanding and aids in better retention.

c. Journaling: Maintain a study journal where you can reflect on what you've learned, jot down questions, and make connections between different topics. Writing can help you internalize the material effectively.

Implementing Active Learning Techniques

Explore active learning strategies, such as discussions, group study, and practical applications, to enhance information retention and understanding.

The Power of Discussions in Active Learning

Discussions are a potent tool for fostering active learning and promoting critical thinking among students. They offer an opportunity for students to articulate their thoughts, share ideas, and engage in a collaborative learning process.

1. Structured Group Discussions: Find a local study group through Meetup or similar, or an online study group that focuses on the material you are studying. ITCertsTraining.com has several study groups you can partake in free as part of the course you purchased. This approach allows for diverse perspectives and promotes active participation from all students.

2. Online Discussion Forums: In the digital age, online platforms provide a space for asynchronous discussions. These forums allow students to engage in meaningful conversations beyond the physical classroom. Students are encouraged to post thoughtful questions, respond to their peers' inquiries, and support their arguments with credible sources. Online discussions extend the learning experience beyond class hours, enabling students to reflect and contribute at their own pace.

3. Debate Sessions: Participate in organized debate sessions where your colleagues take on different roles and argue for or against specific viewpoints related to the subject matter. Debates not only encourage critical thinking but also help develop their persuasion and public speaking skills.

The Impact of Group Study on Active Learning

Group study, also known as collaborative learning, is a powerful technique that enhances active learning through peer interaction and teamwork. When students come together to study, they can benefit from a shared pool of knowledge and expertise. Here's how to make the most of group study sessions:

1. Diverse Group Formation: Find and/or encourage diverse group formations, considering students' different backgrounds, skill sets, and learning styles. A mix of personalities and perspectives can lead to richer discussions and deeper understanding of the subject matter.

2. Clearly Defined Goals: Establish clear objectives for each group study session to maintain focus and direction. Define the topics or concepts to be covered and encourage participants to prepare beforehand to make the discussion more engaging and productive.

3. Rotating Roles: Assign rotating roles within the study groups, such as a facilitator, timekeeper, note-taker, and devil's advocate. By rotating these responsibilities, every student gets a chance to develop various skills and actively contribute to the group's success.

4. Utilize Technology: Embrace technology to facilitate group study, especially if students are geographically dispersed or unable to meet in person. Video conferencing, collaborative online documents, and virtual whiteboards can help maintain an interactive and dynamic group study environment.

Enhancing Active Learning Through Practical Applications

Active learning extends beyond traditional classroom settings; it involves applying knowledge in real-world scenarios. Practical applications enable students to connect theory with practice, making learning more meaningful and memorable. Here are some methods to incorporate practical applications into your teaching approach:

1. Case Studies: Use case studies with real-life scenarios relevant to the subject matter. These scenarios challenge you to analyze situations, identify problems, and propose viable solutions. Through case studies, you develop problem-solving skills and learn to adapt theoretical concepts to real-world complexities.

2. Simulations and Role-Playing: Simulations and role-playing activities allow you to step into different roles and experience situations from various perspectives. Whether it's simulating a historical event, conducting a mock business negotiation, or acting out a computer experiment, these activities foster engagement and experiential learning.

3. Field Trips and Site Visits: If possible, visits to places related to the subject being taught can be very advantageous. Whether it's a museum, a factory, a historical site, or a natural ecosystem, these experiences create lasting impressions and provide tangible connections to the curriculum.

4. Internships and Work Experience: Participate in internships or work experiences relevant to you field of study. Practical exposure in a professional setting can deepen your understanding of concepts, expose you to industry practices, and help you build valuable skills for your future careers.

By incorporating discussions, group study, and practical applications into your study repertoire, you can create an engaging and effective learning environment that nurtures curiosity, critical thinking, and a deeper understanding of the subject matter. These active learning techniques empower you to take ownership of your education and develop the skills needed to thrive in an ever-changing workplace.

Effective Note-Taking Strategies

Master note-taking methods that facilitate comprehension and help you review and revise more efficiently.

Understanding Cornell Notes for Cybersecurity Certification:

Cornell Notes is a widely recognized note-taking system that divides your notes into two sections: the main note-taking section and a summary section. This method encourages active engagement during the lecture or study session, enhancing the learning process and retention.

How to use Cornell Notes for Cybersecurity Certification?

Start by dividing your note-taking paper into two sections: the larger section for taking comprehensive notes and a smaller section for summarizing key points.

During cybersecurity lectures or study sessions, jot down the main ideas, concepts, and important facts in the larger section.

In the summary section, write concise summaries of the key points, making it easier to review and reinforce your understanding later.

After the study session, review and revise your notes regularly to reinforce the information.

The Power of the Outline Method in Cybersecurity Certification Preparation:

The Outline Method involves structuring information hierarchically, organizing ideas into main topics, subtopics, and supporting details. This method helps you see the relationships between different concepts and fosters a logical flow of information.

How to utilize the Outline Method for Cybersecurity Certification?

Create an outline before starting your study session. Identify the main topics that will be covered in your certification exam.

Organize the subtopics and supporting details under each main topic to create a coherent structure.

As you study, fill in the outline with relevant information, ensuring that you understand the connections between different concepts.

Review your outline regularly to reinforce the material and identify areas that need further attention.

Combining Cornell Notes and the Outline Method for Cybersecurity Certification Success:

Create a Cornell Note format for your cybersecurity study sessions:

Label the larger section for main note-taking as "Main Topics" and the smaller section for summarizing as "Summary."

Adopt the Outline Method structure in your "Main Topics" section, organizing the cybersecurity concepts hierarchically.

Take organized and comprehensive notes:

During your cybersecurity study sessions or lectures, fill in the "Main Topics" section with relevant information under the outlined structure.

Utilize bullet points, diagrams, and highlighting to enhance the clarity and visual appeal of your notes.

Summarize and reinforce your understanding:

After each study session, condense the main points from the "Main Topics" section into the "Summary" section using concise language.

Regularly review your summarized notes to reinforce your understanding and identify areas that require further review.

Mastering a cybersecurity certification requires dedication, focus, and efficient study techniques. By combining the power of Cornell Notes and the Outline Method, you can enhance your note-taking process, improve comprehension, and solidify your grasp on essential cybersecurity concepts. Embrace these strategies, and you'll be well on your way to achieving success in your cybersecurity certification journey.

Mind Mapping for Effective Note-Taking

In the previous section, we explored various traditional note-taking methods, such as Cornell Notes and the Outline Method. While these methods are excellent for linear organization and structured information, there are alternative techniques that can enhance creativity, boost comprehension, and foster better memory retention. One such powerful approach is "Mind Mapping." In this section, we will delve into the world of mind mapping for effective note-taking.

What is a Mind Map?

A mind map is a graphical representation of ideas, concepts, and information that visually connects related thoughts, fostering a deeper understanding of the subject matter. Created around a central topic or theme, a mind map branches out into subtopics and further sub-branches, creating a web of interconnected concepts. This method of note-taking harnesses the brain's natural tendency to think associatively, which makes it an ideal technique for brainstorming, planning, and organizing complex information.

Advantages of Mind Mapping

1. Enhanced Creativity: Mind mapping encourages a free flow of ideas and enables connections between seemingly unrelated concepts, stimulating creativity and innovative thinking.

2. Improved Comprehension: By using visual cues and associations, mind maps make it easier to grasp complex topics, helping learners make sense of intricate information.

3. Efficient Review and Revision: The visual nature of mind maps allows for quick and efficient review and revision, as it is easier to identify key points and relationships.

4. Memory Retention: Engaging both the left and right brain hemispheres, mind maps reinforce learning, leading to better memory retention and recall.

Step 1: Start with a Central Idea

To create a mind map, begin with a central idea or topic placed in the center of your page. It can be a keyword, a phrase, or an image representing the main concept of your note-taking session.

Step 2: Add Primary Branches

From the central idea, extend primary branches outward in different directions. Each primary branch represents a key subtopic or category related to the central idea. Use colors, images, and concise keywords to label these branches and make them visually distinct.

Step 3: Expand with Secondary Branches

Next, extend secondary branches from each primary branch to further elaborate on the subtopics. These secondary branches can include more specific details, examples, or related concepts. Continue to use visuals, keywords, and colors to differentiate them from the primary branches.

Step 4: Make Associations

As you build your mind map, look for connections and associations between different branches. Use lines, arrows, or connecting elements to illustrate the relationships between ideas. This is where the true power of mind mapping lies, as it encourages lateral thinking and the exploration of interrelated concepts.

Step 5: Keep it Simple and Clear

While mind maps can be visually captivating, it's essential to maintain simplicity and clarity. Avoid cluttering your map with excessive details or unnecessary information. The purpose is to capture the essence of the topic and its connections.

Mind Mapping Tools

While you can create mind maps using pen and paper, several digital tools can streamline the process and offer additional features. Some popular mind mapping tools include:

1. MindMeister: An online mind mapping tool that allows collaboration and integration with other productivity apps.

2. XMind: A powerful and user-friendly software for creating mind maps, flowcharts, and concept maps.

3. Coggle: An intuitive and collaborative platform for making simple and effective mind maps.

4. MindNode: An app designed specifically for Apple devices, offering a seamless mind mapping experience.

5. Personal Brain: (My favorite!) Flexible, plex oriented, portable, desktop and app based, sharable, unlimited capability and capacity. Simply the best!

Tips for Effective Mind Mapping

1. Use Visuals: Incorporate images, icons, and symbols to reinforce your understanding and make the mind map visually appealing.

2. Practice Regularly: As with any note-taking method, regular practice will refine your mind mapping skills and make the process more natural.

3. Customize Your Style: There's no one-size-fits-all approach to mind mapping. Find a style that works best for you, whether it's colorful and artistic or minimalistic and structured.

4. Review and Revise: After creating a mind map, take the time to review and revise it periodically. This will strengthen your understanding and help you retain information better.

Enhancing Memory and Retention

Discover memory-enhancing techniques and exercises to improve long-term retention of academic material.

(If you are not familiar with Jim Kwik, I suggest you sign up for his free courses. He has a wealth of information about Memory and Retention.)

Memory-Enhancing Techniques and Exercises

In the previous chapter, we explored the importance of memory and its role in academic success. Now, it's time to delve into the practical side of enhancing memory and retention. In this chapter, we will explore various memory-enhancing techniques and exercises that have been proven effective in improving long-term retention of academic material. These techniques can be applied by students, educators, and lifelong learners alike, making the learning process more efficient and enjoyable.

1. Mnemonic Devices: Unlocking the Power of Association

Mnemonic devices are powerful memory aids that use associations to help us remember complex information more easily. These devices work by creating a link between new information and existing knowledge or vivid mental images. There are several types of mnemonic devices, including acronyms, acrostics, rhymes, and visualization.

- Acronyms: Acronyms are formed by taking the first letter of each word in a list and creating a new word from those letters. For example, to remember the order of the planets in our solar system (Mercury, Venus, Earth, Mars, Jupiter, Saturn, Uranus, Neptune), you can use the acronym "My Very Educated Mother Just Served Us Noodles" (MVEMJSUN).

- Acrostics: Similar to acronyms, acrostics use the first letters of words to create a sentence or phrase that helps recall specific information. For instance, to remember the order of operations in mathematics (Parentheses, Exponents, Multiplication, Division, Addition, Subtraction), you can use the acrostic "Please Excuse My Dear Aunt Sally" (PEMDAS).

- Rhymes: Rhymes use a catchy and rhythmic phrase to help remember information. For example, "I before E, except after C, or when sounding like A, as in neighbor or weigh."

- Visualization: Creating vivid mental images can significantly improve memory retention. Visualize the information you want to remember in a memorable and imaginative way. For instance, if you need to remember a list of groceries, picture each item in a specific location of your house.

2. The Method of Loci: Memory Palace Technique

The Method of Loci, also known as the Memory Palace technique, has been used for centuries as a powerful memory-enhancing tool. It involves associating information with specific locations within a familiar environment, such as your home. Here's how you can use this technique:

- Choose a familiar place: Select a location you know well, like your home or a route you frequently take.

- Create a mental journey: Imagine yourself walking through this place in a specific order, noting distinctive features or landmarks at each point.

- Associate information: Associate the information you want to remember with each location in your mental journey.

- Recall with ease: When you need to remember the information, mentally walk through your Memory Palace, and the associated details will come flooding back.

The Method of Loci capitalizes on our spatial memory and the brain's ability to recall information based on the locations where it was stored. It's an effective technique for memorizing lists, speeches, historical timelines, and more.

3. Spaced Repetition: Optimizing Memory Retention

Spaced repetition is a scientifically proven technique that capitalizes on the spacing effect—the phenomenon where information is better retained when it is reviewed at spaced intervals rather than in one long session. This technique is particularly useful for learning new vocabulary, historical dates, formulas, and other discrete pieces of information.

To use spaced repetition effectively:

- Create flashcards: Write a question or cue on one side of the flashcard and the answer on the other side.

- Review with intervals: Start by reviewing the flashcards immediately after creating them. As you review each card, rate your confidence in recalling the information. Cards you are confident about will be reviewed less frequently, while more challenging cards will be reviewed more often.

- Gradually increase intervals: As you become more proficient at recalling the information on each flashcard, space out the intervals between reviews. The goal is to review the material just before you are about to forget it, reinforcing your memory and increasing retention.

4. Chunking: Organizing Information for Improved Recall

Chunking is the process of breaking down large amounts of information into smaller, manageable chunks. By organizing information into meaningful groups, the brain can process and remember more efficiently. This technique is particularly useful for memorizing long strings of numbers, lists, or complex concepts.

For example, try to remember the following string of digits: 849216721906.

It's challenging to recall this sequence in one go. However, if we break it down into chunks: 8492 - 1672 - 1906, it becomes much easier to remember.

When studying, look for patterns or connections between different pieces of information. Group related concepts together, and create mental associations between them. This will not only aid memory but also help in understanding the interconnectedness of the material.

5. Mindful Learning and Meditation: Reducing Cognitive Load

Mindfulness and meditation have been shown to have positive effects on memory and retention. By reducing cognitive load and enhancing focus, these practices enable learners to process and retain information more effectively.

When studying or attending lectures, practice being fully present and attentive to the material. Minimize distractions and engage with the subject matter actively. Mindful learning involves giving your full attention to the task at hand, which can lead to deeper understanding and improved retention.

Similarly, incorporating meditation into your daily routine can have significant benefits for memory enhancement. Meditation helps reduce stress and anxiety, which can otherwise hinder memory consolidation and retrieval.

Conclusion

Enhancing memory and retention is a journey that requires dedication, practice, and the application of various techniques and exercises. By incorporating mnemonic devices, utilizing the Memory Palace technique, leveraging spaced repetition, employing chunking strategies, and embracing mindful learning and meditation, learners can significantly improve their ability to remember and retain academic material.

Remember that everyone's memory capabilities are unique, and finding the techniques that work best for you is key to achieving success. Additionally, combining multiple memory-enhancing techniques can amplify their effectiveness. So, experiment with these techniques, be patient with yourself, and celebrate the progress you make in your quest for an improved memory and a more rewarding academic experience.

Chapter 6: Time Management Techniques for Students

Prioritization Techniques

When it comes to managing time effectively as a student, prioritization is an essential skill that can make a significant difference in your academic performance and overall well-being. Without relying on popular methods like the Eisenhower Matrix or time blocking, let's explore alternative prioritization techniques that can help you stay focused and organized in your studies.

1. ABCD Technique:

The ABCD technique is a simple and effective way to prioritize your tasks based on their importance and urgency. Here's how it works:

- A: Assign the letter A to tasks that are highly important and require immediate attention. These tasks usually have significant consequences if not completed promptly.

- B: Tasks labeled with the letter B are important but not as urgent. They can be postponed for a short while without severe consequences.

- C: Tasks marked with the letter C are nice-to-have but not crucial. If you have spare time after completing A and B tasks, you can work on these.

- D: These tasks are non-essential and can be delegated or eliminated if possible. Focus on A, B, and C tasks before considering D tasks.

By categorizing your tasks using the ABCD technique, you can better allocate your time and energy to address the most critical responsibilities first.

2. MoSCoW Method:

The MoSCoW method is another prioritization technique widely used in project management, but it can be adapted to manage your study tasks effectively:

- Must: Label tasks that are absolutely essential with "Must." These are your top priorities that cannot be delayed or ignored.

- Should: "Should" represents tasks that are important but can be flexibly managed. They have a significant impact, but slight adjustments in their timeline are possible.

- Could: Use "Could" for tasks that are desirable but not vital. They can be addressed if you have ample time or as rewards for completing Must and Should tasks.

- Won't: These are tasks that you have consciously decided not to do. They might be tempting distractions or unrelated activities that don't contribute to your academic goals.

The MoSCoW method helps you streamline your study plan and ensures you focus on what truly matters.

3. Weighted Scoring:

Weighted scoring is a more advanced technique that involves assigning numerical values to each task based on its importance, complexity, and impact on your academic success. Here's how you can use it:

- Identify the criteria: Determine the factors that are important to you, such as deadlines, difficulty level, relevance to exams, etc.

- Assign weights: Assign a numerical weight to each criterion based on its significance. For instance, a project with a closer deadline might get a higher weight.

- Rate tasks: Rate each task based on each criterion and multiply the rating by the corresponding weight. Sum up the scores to get a total score for each task.

- Prioritize tasks: Order your tasks based on their total scores. Higher-scoring tasks should be your focus.

This technique allows for a more personalized approach to prioritization, enabling you to consider multiple factors while managing your time effectively.

4. Value vs. Effort:

This technique involves evaluating tasks based on their value and the effort required to complete them. Here's how to apply it:

- Value: Assess the value or importance of each task in terms of its impact on your academic performance and long-term goals.

- Effort: Estimate the effort and time required to complete each task.

- Plot tasks: Create a graph with "Value" on the x-axis and "Effort" on the y-axis. Place each task on the graph accordingly.

- Focus on high-value, low-effort tasks: Prioritize tasks that fall in the top-left quadrant of the graph, as they offer the most significant return on investment for your time.

By using this technique, you can identify tasks that are worth your attention while avoiding tasks that consume excessive time but yield minimal results.

Conclusion:

Effective time management is crucial for students to maintain a healthy balance between academics and other aspects of life. By employing alternative prioritization techniques like the ABCD method, MoSCoW method, weighted scoring, and value vs. effort analysis, you can optimize your study schedule and achieve better academic results while reducing stress. Experiment with these techniques to find what works best for you and tailor your approach to suit your unique needs and goals.

The Pomodoro Technique: Maximizing Focus

Distractions are everywhere, making it challenging to maintain focus during study sessions. The Pomodoro Technique is a time management method that can help you overcome distractions and improve your concentration, leading to increased productivity in your academic journey.

Understanding the Pomodoro Technique

The Pomodoro Technique was developed by Francesco Cirillo in the late 1980s. It's a simple yet powerful approach that breaks your work into intervals, traditionally 25 minutes in length, separated by short breaks. Here's how it works:

Step 1: Choose a task you want to work on.

Step 2: Set a timer for 25 minutes and commit to focusing solely on that task during this period.

Step 3: Work on the task until the timer rings, avoiding any distractions or interruptions.

Step 4: Take a short break, typically 5 minutes, to rest and recharge.

Step 5: After completing four Pomodoro sessions, take a longer break, around 15-30 minutes, to relax and rejuvenate.

The Pomodoro Technique leverages the concept of "bursts of focused work" followed by short breaks to enhance your mental agility and prevent burnout. By adhering to this structured approach, you can maintain high levels of concentration and productivity.

Advantages of the Pomodoro Technique

Implementing the Pomodoro Technique in your study routine offers several benefits:

1. Improved Focus: Breaking your study time into short intervals helps you concentrate on one task at a time, reducing distractions and enhancing focus.

2. Increased Productivity: The time-bound sessions push you to work efficiently and complete tasks within specific periods, resulting in enhanced productivity.

3. Reduced Procrastination: Knowing you have only a short timeframe to work on a task encourages you to get started and avoid procrastination.

4. Better Time Management: The Pomodoro Technique helps you allocate time for studying, breaks, and other activities, allowing for a well-balanced schedule.

5. Enhanced Retention: Regular breaks give your brain time to consolidate information, improving information retention and recall.

Tips for Implementing the Pomodoro Technique

To make the most of the Pomodoro Technique, consider the following tips:

1. Set Realistic Time Intervals: While traditional Pomodoro sessions are 25 minutes long, feel free to adjust the time intervals to suit your preferences and study habits.

2. Use a Timer: Utilize a timer or one of the many Pomodoro apps available to track your work and break sessions accurately.

3. Create a Distraction-Free Environment: Find a quiet study space where you won't be interrupted during your focused work intervals.

4. Prioritize Tasks: Identify the most critical tasks you need to accomplish and tackle them during your Pomodoro sessions.

5. Stay Flexible: The Pomodoro Technique is a tool to help you, not restrict you. Feel free to adapt the method to your needs as you see fit.

By incorporating the Pomodoro Technique into your study routine, you can maximize your focus and productivity, making your academic journey more efficient and successful.

The Eisenhower Matrix: Sorting Tasks by Importance

In your academic journey, you'll encounter numerous tasks and assignments, each with varying degrees of urgency and importance. The Eisenhower Matrix, also known as the Urgent-Important Matrix (popularized by Stephen Covey's "7 Habits for Highly Successful People"), is a powerful prioritization tool that can help you categorize tasks effectively, ensuring that you focus on what truly matters.

Understanding the Eisenhower Matrix

The Eisenhower Matrix was named after former U.S. President Dwight D. Eisenhower, who famously said, "I have two kinds of problems: the urgent and the important. The urgent are not important, and the important are never urgent."

The matrix classifies tasks into four quadrants based on their urgency and importance:

Quadrant 1: Urgent and Important - Tasks in this quadrant are both urgent and crucial to your academic success. These are your top priorities and require immediate attention.

Quadrant 2: Not Urgent but Important - Tasks in this quadrant are vital for your long-term goals and academic growth but don't require immediate action. They should be scheduled and given ample time for thoughtful execution.

Quadrant 3: Urgent but Not Important - Tasks in this quadrant may demand immediate attention, but they do not contribute significantly to your academic progress. Be cautious not to spend too much time on these tasks as they can be distractions.

Quadrant 4: Not Urgent and Not Important - Tasks in this quadrant are time-wasters and distractions. It's best to eliminate or minimize these activities as much as possible.

Applying the Eisenhower Matrix in Your Academic Journey

To effectively utilize the Eisenhower Matrix, follow these steps:

Step 1: List Your Tasks: Write down all the tasks and assignments you need to complete. Be thorough in capturing everything that requires your attention.

Step 2: Assess Urgency and Importance: For each task, evaluate its urgency and importance. Consider deadlines, potential impact on your grades, and alignment with your academic goals.

Step 3: Categorize Tasks: Place each task into one of the four quadrants based on your assessments.

Step 4: Prioritize Quadrant 1 and 2: Focus on completing tasks in Quadrant 1 (Urgent and Important) first, as these are your top priorities. Then, dedicate time to tasks in Quadrant 2 (Not Urgent but Important) to prevent them from becoming urgent in the future.

Step 5: Minimize Quadrant 3 and 4: Be mindful of spending too much time on tasks in Quadrant 3 (Urgent but Not Important) and eliminate or reduce activities in Quadrant 4 (Not Urgent and Not Important) to optimize your productivity.

Benefits of the Eisenhower Matrix

By using the Eisenhower Matrix, you can experience several advantages:

1. Clear Prioritization: The matrix provides a visual representation of your tasks' importance and urgency, allowing you to make informed decisions about where to focus your efforts.

2. Effective Time Management: By addressing important tasks before they become urgent, you can manage your time more efficiently and reduce stress.

3. Enhanced Productivity: Concentrating on crucial tasks leads to increased productivity and academic performance.

4. Minimized Distractions: Identifying and eliminating or reducing non-essential tasks (Quadrant 3 and 4) helps you stay on track and avoid wasting time.

5. Improved Decision-Making: The Eisenhower Matrix helps you make better decisions about how to allocate your time and energy.

Incorporating the Eisenhower Matrix into your academic life will enable you to prioritize tasks effectively, optimize your time management, and achieve your academic goals more efficiently.

Time Blocking: Structuring Your Day for Success

With a multitude of academic tasks, extracurricular activities, and personal commitments, managing your time effectively becomes crucial to maintaining a healthy balance and achieving success in your academic journey. Time blocking is a powerful scheduling technique that can help you structure your day for maximum efficiency and productivity.

Understanding Time Blocking

Time blocking involves breaking your day into specific blocks or chunks of time, each dedicated to a particular activity or task. By assigning distinct time slots for different activities, you create a structured schedule that allows you to focus solely on the task at hand without distractions or multitasking.

Here's how to implement time blocking effectively:

Step 1: Identify and Prioritize Tasks: Start by listing all the tasks and commitments you need to accomplish in a day. Categorize them based on their urgency and importance.

Step 2: Allocate Time Blocks: Assign dedicated time blocks for each task category. Ensure you allocate sufficient time for essential tasks and avoid overcommitting to prevent burnout.

Step 3: Stick to the Schedule: Once you've created your time blocks, adhere to the schedule as closely as possible. Treat each block as a commitment to help you maintain focus and discipline.

Step 4: Be Realistic and Flexible: While creating your time blocks, be realistic about the time needed for each task. Additionally, be open to adjustments and flexibility, as unexpected events may arise.

Benefits of Time Blocking

Time blocking offers several advantages for your academic journey:

1. Improved Focus: By dedicating specific time blocks to individual tasks, you eliminate distractions and increase your ability to concentrate.

2. Enhanced Time Management: Time blocking ensures you allocate sufficient time for essential activities, preventing procrastination and time wastage.

3. Reduced Stress: With a structured schedule, you can approach each task systematically, reducing the feeling of being overwhelmed.

4. Better Work-Life Balance: By allocating time for both academic and personal activities, you can maintain a healthy balance between your studies and personal life.

5. Increased Productivity: The focused and dedicated approach of time blocking leads to higher productivity and efficiency.

Tips for Effective Time Blocking

To make the most of time blocking, consider the following tips:

1. Set Realistic Goals: Avoid overloading your schedule with too many tasks. Set achievable goals for each time block to maintain a sense of accomplishment.

2. Include Breaks: Incorporate short breaks between time blocks to rest and recharge, promoting sustained focus throughout the day.

3. Leverage Productivity Tools: Utilize productivity apps, calendars, or planners to help you organize and manage your time effectively.

4. Review and Adjust: Regularly assess your time blocking strategy to identify areas for improvement and make necessary adjustments.

5. Be Consistent: Stick to your time-blocking routine consistently to develop a habit that enhances your productivity over time.

In conclusion, time blocking is a valuable technique to structure your day, improve your time management skills, and boost productivity in your academic journey. By combining time blocking with other prioritization techniques like the Pomodoro Technique and the Eisenhower Matrix, you can create a powerful system for achieving your academic goals and excelling in your studies.

Chapter 7: Overcoming Procrastination

The Psychology of Procrastination

Procrastination is a prevalent challenge that many students face when it comes to their academic performance. Understanding the underlying psychological reasons for procrastination can help you gain insights into your own behavior and take steps to overcome it effectively.

The Comfort of Instant Gratification: **Procrastination often stems from a** mis-represented desire for instant gratification. We tend to prioritize short-term pleasures, such as scrolling through social media, watching videos, or engaging in other leisure activities, over long-term goals like studying for exams or completing assignments. These "habits" of distracitons are fueled by dopamine hits to our brain. Learning to recondition how our brain responds to dopamine can be a powerful transformation in ones life. By recognizing this inclination, you can start to rewire your brain to find satisfaction, not just in completing important tasks, but in truly achieving your real desires in life.

Fear of Failure and Perfectionism: **Fear of failure can be a powerful** driver of procrastination. When you fear that your efforts won't meet your own high standards or the expectations of others, you may subconsciously delay starting a task to avoid potential disappointment. Embracing the idea that mistakes and setbacks are a natural part of the learning process can help alleviate this fear and encourage you to take action.

Lack of Task Clarity: **Sometimes, procrastination arises from a lack of** clarity about the task at hand. When a task seems overwhelming or ambiguous, it's easier to put it off until later. Breaking tasks down into smaller, manageable steps and creating a clear plan can make it less daunting and provide a sense of direction.

Avoidance of Discomfort: **Procrastination can also be a coping** mechanism to avoid discomfort or unpleasant emotions associated with certain tasks. Whether it's boredom, frustration, or anxiety, these feelings can be challenging to confront. Developing emotional resilience and learning to cope with these emotions can make it easier to face tasks head-on.

Identifying Procrastination Patterns

I recommend finding a good Coach to guide you through this. You can use the Habit Finder Assessment mentioned above as a means to help you. Therapy or counselling is rarely useful or needed to deal with procrastination.

To effectively combat procrastination, it's essential to recognize common patterns and personal triggers that lead to avoidance behaviors. Identifying these patterns can help you develop strategies to prevent procrastination from interfering with your studies.

Recognizing Procrastination Behaviors: **Start by observing your behavior** when it comes to studying or completing academic tasks. Do you find yourself delaying important tasks by engaging in less important activities? Are you consistently putting off specific subjects or assignments? Understanding your patterns of avoidance is the first step in overcoming them.

Tracking Time Management: **Keeping a journal or using time-tracking** apps can be beneficial in understanding how you allocate your time. It can reveal patterns of inefficiency and highlight moments when procrastination takes over. Analyzing this data can provide valuable insights into your time management habits.

Identifying Triggers: **Personal triggers can vary from individual to** individual. For some, it might be a particular environment that promotes distraction, such as a noisy room or cluttered workspace. For others, it might be the fear of failure, which hampers their ability to start a task. Pinpointing these triggers empowers you to create a proactive approach to counteract them.

Seeking Feedback: **Sometimes, others can recognize patterns of** procrastination in us that we might overlook. Again, a good Coach is very useful here. Otherwise, ask friends, family members, or study partners for honest feedback about your study habits. Their insights can offer valuable perspectives on areas you need to improve.

Strategies to Beat Procrastination

Now that you have a deeper understanding of the psychological aspects of procrastination and have identified your own patterns and triggers, it's time to explore practical strategies to overcome procrastination and establish a consistent study routine.

The Two-Minute Rule: **Often, the hardest part of starting a task is the** initial resistance. The two-minute rule suggests committing to working on a task for just two minutes. Once you start, you may find that it's easier to continue than you initially thought.

Create a Study Schedule: **Develop a detailed study schedule that** includes specific time blocks for each subject or task. Set realistic goals for what you want to achieve during those study sessions. A well-structured schedule can create a sense of accountability and provide a clear roadmap for your studies.

Use Time Management Techniques: **Employ time management** techniques such as the Pomodoro Technique, where you work for a focused 25-minute period and then take a short break. This approach can help you maintain concentration and productivity while reducing the feeling of being overwhelmed.

Reward Yourself: **Create a system of rewards for completing tasks or** achieving study goals. Treat yourself to a favorite snack, short break, or enjoyable activity as a way to reinforce positive behavior and create positive associations with studying.

Eliminate Distractions: **Identify common distractions and take measures** to minimize their impact. Turn off social media notifications, find a quiet study space, or use website blockers to limit access to time-wasting websites during study sessions.

Cultivating Discipline and Willpower

Beating procrastination and maintaining a consistent study routine require cultivating discipline and strengthening your willpower. These are valuable skills that extend beyond academics and can benefit various aspects of your life.

Set Clear Goals: **Clearly define your academic goals and the reasons** why you want to achieve them. Having a strong sense of purpose will fuel your motivation and make it easier to stay disciplined.

Practice Self-Compassion: **Acknowledge that nobody is perfect, and** occasional slip-ups are normal. Be kind to yourself when you face challenges, and instead of dwelling on past procrastination, focus on learning from it and moving forward.

Build Habits Gradually: **Trying** to overhaul your study habits overnight can be overwhelming and unsustainable. Instead, focus on building one positive habit at a time. Once it becomes ingrained, move on to the next one.

Visualize Success: Imagine yourself succeeding in your academic pursuits. Visualization can be a powerful tool to boost motivation and reinforce your commitment to overcoming procrastination.

Surround Yourself with Support: **Share** your goals and progress with friends, family, or study partners who can provide encouragement and accountability. Having a support system can make the journey to conquer procrastination less lonely and more rewarding.

Remember that overcoming procrastination is a process that requires patience and persistence. Celebrate your small victories and stay committed to your academic journey. By understanding the psychology of procrastination, identifying your patterns, and implementing effective strategies, you can cultivate discipline, improve your study habits, and achieve academic excellence.

Chapter 8: Maintaining Motivation and Momentum

Celebrating Your Achievements

Congratulations! You've embarked on an exciting journey to earn your certification, and it's essential to acknowledge and celebrate your achievements along the way. In this chapter, we will explore the significance of celebrating milestones and progress during your certification preparation. Recognizing your accomplishments will not only boost your motivation but also help maintain the momentum needed to stay focused on your goal.

Why Celebrating Matters

Studying for a certification is a challenging endeavor that requires dedication, time, and effort. As you progress through your studies, it's easy to get overwhelmed by the amount of material to cover and the complexity of the topics. Celebrating your achievements, no matter how small, is a powerful way to combat feelings of burnout and maintain a positive attitude throughout your journey.

When you celebrate your successes, you trigger a positive feedback loop in your brain. This loop reinforces the idea that your hard work and dedication are paying off, making you more likely to continue putting in the effort. Additionally, celebrating your progress provides a well-deserved break from the intensity of studying, allowing you to recharge and return to your studies with renewed energy.

Ways to Celebrate Your Achievements

Milestone Rewards: Set up a reward system for reaching specific milestones in your certification journey. For example, after completing a challenging chapter or practice exam, treat yourself to something you enjoy, like a favorite meal, a movie night, or a small gift.

Study Group Celebrations: If you're studying with a group of friends or colleagues, celebrate each other's achievements together. Acknowledge the progress made by each member and motivate each other to keep going.

Personal Notes and Journaling: Take a moment to write down your achievements and what they mean to you. Keeping a journal of your progress allows you to reflect on how far you've come and reminds you of your determination when facing future challenges.

Social Media Sharing: Share your progress on social media platforms to receive support and encouragement from friends, family, or even fellow cybersecurity enthusiasts. Their positive comments can be a great source of motivation.

Rewarding Learning Breaks: While studying, allow yourself short breaks to do something enjoyable, like going for a walk, playing a quick game, or listening to your favorite music. These mini-celebrations can refresh your mind and prevent burnout.

Visualization and Affirmations: Take a few moments daily to visualize yourself successfully obtaining your certification. Repeat positive affirmations to boost your confidence and motivation.

The Power of Gratitude

Gratitude plays a significant role in maintaining motivation and momentum during your certification journey. Take a moment each day to appreciate the progress you've made and the opportunities that lie ahead. Gratitude shifts your focus from what you lack to what you have achieved, instilling a positive mindset that enhances your ability to persevere through challenges.

Challenges and Overcoming Setbacks

While celebrating achievements is crucial, it's also essential to acknowledge that challenges and setbacks are a natural part of the learning process. Some days might be more challenging than others, and you may encounter topics that seem particularly difficult to grasp. During these moments, remember that setbacks are temporary, and with persistence, you can overcome them.

If you find yourself stuck or facing a particularly challenging topic, consider seeking help from online forums, study groups, or instructors. Don't be afraid to ask questions or request clarification—there's no shame in seeking guidance. Remember that you are not alone on this journey, and others have likely faced similar challenges.

Celebrating your achievements and milestones during your cybersecurity certification journey is crucial for maintaining motivation and momentum. Acknowledging your progress, both big and small, reinforces your dedication and keeps you focused on the end goal. Remember that setbacks are normal, and with a positive mindset and a support network, you can overcome them. Stay committed, stay positive, and keep celebrating your success throughout this fulfilling journey towards becoming a certified cybersecurity professional.

Tracking Progress and Making Adjustments

When it comes to studying for your cybersecurity certification, maintaining motivation and momentum is crucial. It's a challenging journey that requires dedication and perseverance. In this chapter, we will explore the importance of tracking your progress and making necessary adjustments to stay on course and achieve your certification goals.

Tracking Your Progress:

Set Clear Milestones: Breaking down your study plan into smaller, achievable milestones can help you stay focused and motivated. Create a study schedule with specific targets for each week or month, and celebrate your accomplishments as you reach each milestone.

Use Study Logs: Keep a study log to record the topics you cover each day, the resources you use, and the time you spend studying. This log will not only help you track your progress but also identify any patterns or areas where you might need to invest more time and effort.

Practice with Mock Exams: Take advantage of practice exams and mock tests. They can give you a clear picture of your current knowledge level, highlight areas of weakness, and simulate the actual exam environment. Regularly review your scores to monitor improvement over time.

Utilize Online Tools: There are numerous online tools and apps available that can help you track your study progress. They offer features like study reminders, progress analytics, and goal-setting capabilities, making it easier to stay organized and motivated.

Seek Feedback: If you're studying with a group or under the guidance of an instructor, don't hesitate to ask for feedback on your performance. Constructive criticism can help you understand your strengths and weaknesses and guide you in making improvements.

Making Necessary Adjustments:

Identify Problem Areas: **Analyze** your study log and mock exam results to identify subjects or topics where you are struggling. Understanding your weak points will enable you to focus your efforts on those areas and seek additional resources or assistance if needed.

Adjust Your Study Plan: **Be** flexible with your study plan. If you find that certain topics require more time than expected, adjust your schedule accordingly. Additionally, if you notice that your current study methods are not yielding desired results, try different approaches and learning techniques.

Reevaluate Time Management: **Time** management is crucial when studying for a certification exam. If you're struggling to find enough time to study, reevaluate your daily routine, and identify areas where you can allocate more time to your studies. Eliminate distractions and prioritize your learning.

Stay Positive and Persistent: **It's** normal to face challenges and setbacks while preparing for a cybersecurity certification. Stay positive and persistent throughout the process. Celebrate your achievements, no matter how small, and use any setbacks as learning opportunities to improve.

Join Study Groups or Forums: **Interacting** with others who are also studying for the same certification can be incredibly motivating. Join online study groups or forums where you can discuss concepts, share resources, and get support from like-minded individuals.

Take Breaks and Practice Self-Care: **Avoid** burnout by taking regular breaks during your study sessions. Engage in activities that help you relax and recharge, such as exercise, meditation, or spending time with friends and family. A refreshed mind is more receptive to learning.

Tracking your progress and making necessary adjustments are fundamental aspects of maintaining motivation and momentum while studying for your cybersecurity certification. By setting clear milestones, utilizing study logs, practicing with mock exams, and being open to adjustments, you can stay on track and increase your chances of success. Remember that the journey to certification might be challenging, but with dedication and the right approach, you can overcome obstacles and achieve your goals. Stay focused, stay motivated, and keep pushing forward!

Embracing a Growth Mindset

Studying for a certification requires dedication, commitment, and a growth mindset. In this chapter, we will explore the concept of a growth mindset and how it can significantly impact your motivation and momentum throughout your certification preparation. By adopting a growth mindset, you'll be better equipped to overcome challenges, stay persistent, and ultimately achieve success in your cybersecurity certification journey.

Understanding the Growth Mindset:

The concept of a growth mindset was popularized by psychologist Carol Dweck. In contrast to a fixed mindset, where individuals believe their abilities are innate and unchangeable, a growth mindset is the belief that talents and abilities can be developed through dedication, hard work, and perseverance. Embracing a growth mindset is crucial when studying for a cybersecurity certification because it helps you approach challenges and setbacks as opportunities for learning and improvement.

Benefits of a Growth Mindset in Cybersecurity Certification:

Resilience in the Face of Challenges: **Studying for a cybersecurity certification is a demanding task that may involve complex technical concepts and extensive practical exercises. With a growth mindset, you'll view challenges as stepping stones to improvement, allowing you to bounce back from setbacks with renewed determination.**

Embracing Continuous Learning: **The field of cybersecurity is constantly evolving, with new threats and technologies emerging regularly. A growth mindset encourages you to embrace continuous learning, staying updated with the latest trends and best practices even after you obtain your certification.**

Increased Effort and Persistence: **When you believe that your efforts can lead to improvement, you're more likely to invest time and energy into your studies. This increased effort and persistence will propel you forward and keep you motivated even during challenging study sessions.**

Strategies to Develop a Growth Mindset:

Embrace the Learning Process: Instead of solely focusing on the end goal of passing the certification exam, appreciate the learning journey itself. Break down the material into smaller, manageable chunks and celebrate each milestone you achieve along the way.

Reframe "Failures" as Learning Opportunities: In the cybersecurity field, you may encounter scenarios where you don't immediately grasp a concept or make mistakes in practice exercises. Instead of being discouraged, see these moments as opportunities to learn and grow. Analyze what went wrong, understand the underlying concepts, and use this knowledge to improve.

Seek Support and Feedback: Surround yourself with a supportive community of fellow learners, mentors, or cybersecurity professionals. Engage in discussions, seek feedback on your progress, and learn from others' experiences. This support network will keep you motivated and accountable.

Visualize Success: Envision yourself succeeding in your cybersecurity career after obtaining the certification. Visualizing positive outcomes can reinforce your commitment to the process and boost your motivation to study consistently.

Adopting a growth mindset is a powerful tool that can propel you forward on your journey to certification success. Embrace the idea that you can continuously improve and develop the necessary skills to thrive in this dynamic and essential field. Remember that setbacks are a natural part of the learning process, and with a growth mindset, you can turn challenges into opportunities for growth and advancement. Stay persistent, maintain your motivation, and let your growth mindset be the driving force that helps you achieve your certification goals.

Seeking Support and Accountability

Congratulations on embarking on your journey to earn your cybersecurity certification! Studying for a certification in this field can be a challenging but immensely rewarding experience. As you progress through your preparation, you may encounter moments of doubt, fatigue, and the temptation to give up. In this chapter, we will explore the importance of seeking support and accountability to stay motivated and maintain momentum throughout your cybersecurity certification journey.

Join Study Groups and Forums

One of the most effective ways to stay motivated and maintain momentum is by joining study groups or online forums dedicated to cybersecurity certification preparation. These groups provide an excellent platform to connect with like-minded individuals who are also on the same path as you. You can share your experiences, exchange study tips, and seek help when facing challenges. Additionally, participating in discussions and helping others in the group can reinforce your knowledge and boost your confidence.

Find a Study Buddy

Studying alone can sometimes be overwhelming, but having a study buddy can make the journey more enjoyable and productive. Look for someone with a similar level of dedication and commitment to cybersecurity certification. Studying together allows you to motivate each other, keep each other accountable, and celebrate milestones together. You can also engage in friendly competitions and quizzes to make learning more engaging.

Online Learning Platforms and Courses

Many online learning platforms offer cybersecurity courses and resources, complete with study schedules, quizzes, and interactive content. Enrolling in these courses not only provides structure to your preparation but also connects you with a community of learners. Additionally, some platforms have discussion forums where you can interact with instructors and other students, creating a sense of belonging and accountability.

Set Clear Goals and Milestones

Defining clear goals and milestones is essential to maintain motivation and momentum. Break down your cybersecurity certification journey into smaller, achievable objectives. Celebrate each milestone you reach, whether it's completing a specific module, achieving a certain score on a practice exam, or mastering a particular concept. Acknowledging your progress will boost your confidence and drive you forward.

Track Your Progress

Keeping track of your study progress can be an excellent way to stay motivated. Use a study journal or a digital tool to record the topics you've covered, the areas you've improved in, and the ones you need to revisit. Tracking your progress visually provides a sense of accomplishment and helps you identify patterns or areas that require more attention.

Visualize Success

Visualization is a powerful technique to maintain motivation. Close your eyes and imagine yourself successfully passing the cybersecurity certification exam. Picture the moment you receive your certificate, the sense of pride and accomplishment you'll feel, and the opportunities that will open up for your career. Use this mental image as fuel to keep pushing forward, especially during challenging moments.

Reward Yourself

Give yourself small rewards for completing study sessions or reaching specific milestones. Treat yourself to something you enjoy, like a favorite snack, a short break for a hobby, or a leisure activity. These rewards act as positive reinforcements and make your study journey more enjoyable.

Stay Positive and Persistent

Staying positive and maintaining a persistent mindset is crucial throughout your cybersecurity certification preparation. You may encounter setbacks or encounter topics that seem difficult at first, but remember that every challenge is an opportunity to learn and grow. Embrace a growth mindset, and don't be too hard on yourself. With determination and perseverance, you can overcome any obstacles.

Seeking support and accountability can significantly impact your motivation and momentum while studying for your cybersecurity certification. Engaging with study groups, finding a study buddy, enrolling in online courses, setting clear goals, tracking progress, visualizing success, rewarding yourself, and maintaining a positive and persistent mindset are essential strategies for success. Embrace the journey, stay committed, and remember that achieving your cybersecurity certification is not just about the destination but also about the knowledge and skills you gain along the way. Happy studying!

Conclusion

In this book, we have explored the vital concepts of time management and goal setting to enhance studying and learning. By understanding the significance of effective time management, you can optimize your study schedule and achieve better results in less time. Setting SMART goals ensures that your objectives are clear, attainable, and time-bound, providing you with a sense of direction and purpose in your academic journey.

We've discussed the impact of your study environment on your focus and productivity, emphasizing the importance of organizing your study space and minimizing distractions. Developing effective study habits, tailored to your learning style, enables you to absorb information efficiently and retain knowledge for the long term.

Moreover, we've introduced various time management techniques, such as prioritization, the Pomodoro Technique, the Eisenhower Matrix, and time blocking, which will help you make the most of your study sessions and achieve a healthy work-life balance.

Overcoming procrastination is a crucial aspect of effective time management and goal setting. By identifying procrastination patterns and adopting strategies to beat them, you can ensure consistent progress towards your academic objectives.

Finally, we've explored ways to maintain motivation and momentum throughout your learning journey. Celebrating achievements, tracking progress, embracing a growth mindset, and seeking support and accountability all play a significant role in keeping you motivated and focused on your goals.

Action Plan

To put the principles discussed in this eBook into action, follow this step-by-step action plan:

1. Conduct a Time Management Self-Assessment: Reflect on your current time management skills and identify areas for improvement.

2. Set SMART Goals: Define clear and achievable goals for your studies, ensuring they adhere to the SMART criteria.

3. Organize Your Study Environment: Create a conducive study space that minimizes distractions and maximizes focus.

4. Develop Effective Study Habits: Identify your learning style and implement active learning techniques and note-taking strategies that suit your preferences.

5. Apply Time Management Techniques: Experiment with prioritization, the Pomodoro Technique, the Eisenhower Matrix, and time blocking to optimize your study schedule.

6. Overcome Procrastination: Recognize and address procrastination patterns using the strategies provided in this eBook.

7. Maintain Motivation and Momentum: Celebrate your achievements, track your progress, and seek support to stay motivated and accountable.

Remember, effective time management and goal setting are skills that require practice and refinement. Be patient with yourself as you incorporate these strategies into your daily routine, and remember that small, consistent steps can lead to significant progress over time.

Best of luck on your journey towards enhanced studying and learning! Remember, with dedication and the right approach, you can achieve your academic goals and unlock your full potential. Keep striving for excellence, and the rewards will follow.

References

1. Covey, S. R. (1989). The 7 Habits of Highly Effective People: Powerful Lessons in Personal Change. Simon & Schuster.

2. Tracy, B. (2007). Eat That Frog!: 21 Great Ways to Stop Procrastinating and Get More Done in Less Time. Berrett-Koehler Publishers.

3. Duhigg, C. (2012). The Power of Habit: Why We Do What We Do in Life and Business. Random House.

4. Allen, D. (2015). Getting Things Done: The Art of Stress-Free Productivity. Penguin.

5. Pink, D. H. (2018). When: The Scientific Secrets of Perfect Timing. Riverhead Books.

6. Duckworth, A. L. (2016). Grit: The Power of Passion and Perseverance. Scribner.

7. Oakley, B. (2014). A Mind for Numbers: How to Excel at Math and Science (Even If You Flunked Algebra). TarcherPerigee.

8. Medina, J. (2008). Brain Rules: 12 Principles for Surviving and Thriving at Work, Home, and School. Pear Press.

9. Locke, E. A., & Latham, G. P. (2002). Building a practically useful theory of goal setting and task motivation: A 35-year odyssey. American Psychologist, 57(9), 705-717.

10. Duckworth, A. L., Peterson, C., Matthews, M. D., & Kelly, D. R. (2007). Grit: Perseverance and passion for long-term goals. Journal of Personality and Social Psychology, 92(6), 1087-1101.

11. Deci, E. L., & Ryan, R. M. (1985). Intrinsic motivation and self-determination in human behavior. Springer Science & Business Media.

12. Pink, D. H. (2009). Drive: The Surprising Truth About What Motivates Us. Riverhead Books.

13. Tuckman, B. W. (1991). The development and concurrent validity of the Procrastination Scale. Educational and Psychological Measurement, 51(2), 473-480.

14. Fiore, N. A. (2006). The Now Habit: A Strategic Program for Overcoming Procrastination and Enjoying Guilt-Free Play. Penguin.

15. Csikszentmihalyi, M. (1991). Flow: The Psychology of Optimal Experience. Harper & Row.

Remember to cite specific sources within the text whenever you use information or quotes from the referenced materials.